Learning Centers
Getting Them Started, Keeping Them Going

Copyright © 1994 by Michael F. Opitz
Cover and interior design by Vincent Ceci
Cover illustration by Drew Hires
Interior illustration by Drew Hires and Carmen Robert Sorvillo
0-590-49554-2
Printed in U.S.A.

12 11 10 9 8   0 1 2/0

Learning Centers
Getting Them Started, Keeping Them Going
Michael F. Opitz

SCHOLASTIC
PROFESSIONAL BOOKS

New York • Toronto • London • Sydney • Auckland

ACKNOWLEDGMENTS

While this book bears my name, it is the result of a collaborative effort among several individuals. I would like to acknowledge each of them.

To Susan Womack-Closset, Scholastic representative, for suggesting that I submit the manuscript.

To Terry Cooper, Editor-in-Chief, Scholastic Professional Books, for her insight, enthusiasm, support, and encouragement.

To Joan Novelli, editor, for her valuable suggestions and for making an arduous task easier.

To Helen Moore Sorvillo, editor, for transforming the original manuscript into the book in its present form and for her sensitivity and humor.

To Mary Beth Spann, writer, for her input and ideas.

To Margaret Ballantyne, teacher, for reviewing and providing comments and suggestions on an earlier version of this manuscript.

To Kelly Anaya, Rich Avina, Donna Cooper, Dena Giglio, Teresa Huff, Patti Lampe, Vonda Lane, Martha Poole, and Debbie Wolfe for contributing photographs of their centers.

To my many students who helped me to clarify the essentials of learning centers.

To teachers who have inspired me, and to those who inspire others.

To Sheryl, my wife, for her patience and support from start to finish.

To all those who continue to believe in me.

Table of Contents

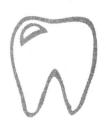

Introduction

I 've tried using Learning Centers but they just don't seem to work for me. How do you get them to work so well?"

My colleague's question caught me unprepared. "Thanks, but I'm not sure I'm as successful as you may think," I remember saying, fumbling for an answer. Truth be told, I was new to the idea and felt like I was charting unknown waters. I had a vision of how I wanted my classroom to look and feel and, while my colleague viewed me as a success, I knew that I had yet to achieve my goal. Her question made me realize, though, that I was so focused on the challenges and frustrations—getting students to work with one another, motivating them to take more responsibility for their learning, finding and creating materials to use in the centers, keeping the classroom from becoming total chaos—that I hadn't taken time to look at what was going well and to reflect on what I had already accomplished.

Reflect is exactly what the question made me do and the result is what this book is about—implementing learning centers successfully. In the pages that follow, you'll find a framework for creating and using learning centers that meet your instructional goals—and match your teaching style. Throughout the book, you'll find answers to the questions asked most, including: "What do I do day one?" A five-day plan helps you through that first day—and the rest of the week.

I have found, and I suspect that you will too, that students need to be taught how to work in a learning centered environment. You may want to conduct short lessons related to specific procedures. Strategies for developing these lessons, as well as ready-to-use mini-lessons on such topics as caring for materials and rotating chaos-free from center to center, are included to assist you. You'll also find:

- suggested center topics,
- ideas for each month,
- "topic bursts" that show how you can establish a basic framework that provides for change within the structure, and
- ready-to-use center activities, complete with student directions

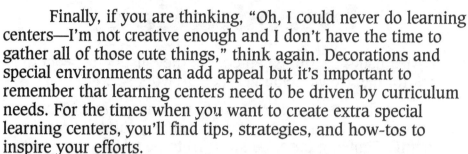

Finally, if you are thinking, "Oh, I could never do learning centers—I'm not creative enough and I don't have the time to gather all of those cute things," think again. Decorations and special environments can add appeal but it's important to remember that learning centers need to be driven by curriculum needs. For the times when you want to create extra special learning centers, you'll find tips, strategies, and how-tos to inspire your efforts.

As you begin implementing centers, keep in mind that, like our students, we need to experience success. This success is what gives us the motivation and courage to stick with an idea and is what encourages us to continue to learn and to refine what we have learned. Yes, you may experience some frustrations as you begin to use centers. I have found that this is usually the case when I try something new because I have to alter my way of thinking, often easier said than done. Remember to take time to celebrate your successes and to give yourself credit for taking the risk to try something new.

—Michael F. Opitz

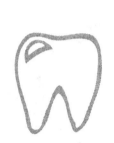

PART ONE
Getting Them Started

Chapter 1

Thinking Through Learning Centers
The whats, whys, and hows of using learning
centers in your classroom
Page 11-18

Chapter 2

Setting Up for Success
Design options for your classroom, a checklist and
floor plan to reproduce, strategies for grouping and
scheduling students, plus suggestions for
managing materials
Page 19-32

Chapter 3

Assessment Options
Adapting your assessment plan for learning
centers, including reproducible teacher and
student evaluation forms
Pages 33-46

CHAPTER 1

Thinking Through Learning Centers

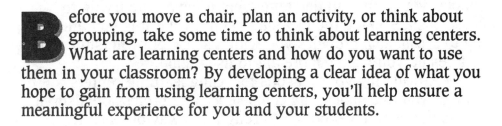
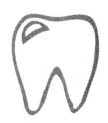

Before you move a chair, plan an activity, or think about grouping, take some time to think about learning centers. What are learning centers and how do you want to use them in your classroom? By developing a clear idea of what you hope to gain from using learning centers, you'll help ensure a meaningful experience for you and your students.

What Is a Learning Center?

When I first started exploring learning centers, I discovered many terms used interchangeably with learning centers, for example: learning stations, activity time, free choice, and interest centers. With each came a different definition, causing some confusion at the onset. I soon realized, though, that there was no one definition of a learning center.

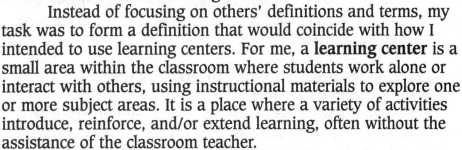

Instead of focusing on others' definitions and terms, my task was to form a definition that would coincide with how I intended to use learning centers. For me, a **learning center** is a small area within the classroom where students work alone or interact with others, using instructional materials to explore one or more subject areas. It is a place where a variety of activities introduce, reinforce, and/or extend learning, often without the assistance of the classroom teacher.

As you reflect on your instructional needs and your vision for your classroom, you'll start to see the range of possibilities in learning centers and to develop your own definition of learning centers, which may be a variation of the one I've shared here.

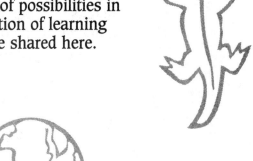

Why Use Learning Centers?

"Because they're fun!" is the first comment that pops into my mind. Learning centers encourage you to be a facilitator in the learning process instead of a "sage on stage" all day, every day. Spontaneous responses aside, this question is important to ask and answer for several reasons.

• Being able to state why you want to use learning centers enables you to fully understand what it is you are trying to accomplish. Seeking the meaning behind what it is you are trying to accomplish provides you with a sense of ownership and, as a result, you will be more apt to use them.

• Articulating your reasons for using learning centers enables you to demonstrate competence and professionalism. It shows that you have thought through this way of teaching rather than simply adding a new idea.

• Having specific reasons for using learning centers helps on those days when little seems to go as planned. They can pull you back on course and motivate you to continue.

As a result of my own experience and a lot of reading, I have accumulated a collection of sound reasons for using learning centers. To give you a start on identifying your own reasons, twelve of those reasons are shared here. The first four focus on the learners, the second four on the teacher, and the remaining four on the overall structure.

1. To enable learners to work in various groups, same and mixed ability.

As students work with various groups and are assigned team leader roles in turn, they develop greater understanding of self and others, increased friendliness toward others, and leadership skills. There is also increased learning as a result of increased expectations and help from others. Less stigma attached to given ability levels.

2. To encourage active participation among all learners.

Because activities require students to be engaged from the minute they arrive until it's time to leave, more learning can occur at a faster rate. You may also experience fewer discipline problems because students are so engaged in their learning.

3. To enable learners to make decisions, follow directions, work independently, and evaluate themselves.

Designing centers with choices encourages a feeling of ownership in the learning process and gives students opportunities to learn responsibility and organization as they select and follow through on the activities they choose.

4. To give students an opportunity to learn responsibility and organization.

Because students are taught how to care for materials and they are expected to do so, their feelings of self-confidence and ownership swell.

5. To facilitate individualized learning.

A variety of open-ended activities and tasks makes individualization more manageable and maximizes learning for each student.

6. To enable individual and small-group instruction.

Students can work independently and in groups, using each other as resources to help solve problems. There is a potential for a greater amount of learning. Students are encouraged to share their strengths with others (rather than having students wait for you). You can provide needed instruction to other students with minimal amount of interruptions.

7. To gain more information about students.

As students work independently, you can circulate and observe the skills, work habits, attitudes, and interests of students as they complete various center activities. The result? Better understanding of student strengths and needs and a wealth of information for individualizing instruction.

8. To incorporate student interests when planning instruction.

Using devices such as student surveys, you can design centers that reflect students' interests and encourage students to see learning as a meaningful, rewarding activity. Greater attention to tasks and increased learning will naturally follow.

9. To provide for various learning styles.

Centers that include a variety of tasks with attention to modalities increase learning with minimal frustration.

10. To provide opportunities for cooperative learning experiences.

Activities that require students to work with one another offer increased gains for all learners, especially students who may not have a chance to shine in more traditional settings.

11. To provide a structure that integrates language and content learning.

By designing content centers that require language use in one or more forms, you can help students see language as a communication tool rather than an end in and of itself, and facilitate language growth for all learners.

12. To make better use of resources.

Fewer students use core materials at a given time; therefore, not as many of any one are needed. You can purchase more materials thereby providing a wider variety to meet varying abilities and interests.

Ways to Use Learning Centers

When I asked myself how I wanted to use learning centers, I had to think through some ways centers can be used and the potential advantages and disadvantages associated with each approach. I also found it

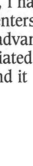

helpful to refer back to my overall reasons for wanting to use centers. There's no one right way to use centers, but as you formulate your reasons for using learning centers, the following options can help you find a way that best supports your goals:

To append the curriculum: When learning centers are used this way, students are permitted to go to centers when and if they have time; other assigned work comes first. A potential advantage for using centers this way is that they provide an added incentive for some students to finish certain tasks. A disadvantage is that often times several students never get to the centers for one reason or another. These are often the same children who might benefit the most from using the centers. Another disadvantage is that some students might complete assignments in a hurried manner, their focus being on finishing rather than learning, their goal being getting to centers.

To extend learners' abilities to make choices: When used in this manner, students are offered a given number of centers from which to choose during a scheduled time in the day, sometimes called free choice or activity time. All students are expected to choose a center, complete the activity, and to clean up the area before choosing the next center. Students are also often expected to keep a record of the centers they complete. The fact that all students have the opportunity to participate is a major advantage for this approach to using centers. One disadvantage, though, is classroom size: There simply may not be enough room to set up enough centers to accommodate all learners.

To organize and deliver all or part of the curriculum: With this plan, students learn a major part of the curriculum by working at centers throughout the day. Because the curriculum is delivered through the centers, students are required to go to each and to complete specified activities. One major advantage is that some aspects of the curriculum are easier to teach using this approach.

Take art. Having one group of students paint in an area close to the sink is easier than having an entire class paint at one time. Centers are advantageous in science, as well. If you're using microscopes or other expensive equipment, for example, you probably don't have a class set. Rather than crowd students around three or four, students can have plenty of time to explore in learning centers.

One disadvantage has to do with time. Some centers may not take as long as others to complete, leaving some students with idle hands until there is room at another center. Likewise, not all students work at the same rate, leaving some students ready to move on while students at the next center are still working. (For ways to deal with this disadvantage, see page 88.)

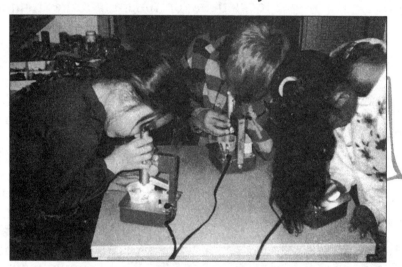

A Plan Emerges

With these options and my aforementioned reasons for wanting to use centers in mind, I decided to use learning centers

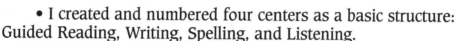

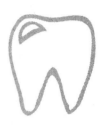

as a way to organize the language arts curriculum and as a way to integrate the language arts with other content areas. Here's how I did it:

- I created and numbered four centers as a basic structure: Guided Reading, Writing, Spelling, and Listening.
- I changed activities within the centers depending on specific objectives, student needs, and interests. Most often, one center was teacher directed, the others student directed.
- All students were required to go to the centers because this is how they acquired much of the curriculum.
- I created a fifth center and called it free choice. This center housed open-ended activities that students could complete if they were finished with one center and waiting to go to the next. This center was usually optional. However, there were some days when I skipped one of the other centers and required students to go to the free choice center. This offered another opportunity for learning how to make and follow through on choices.

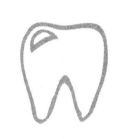

CHAPTER 2

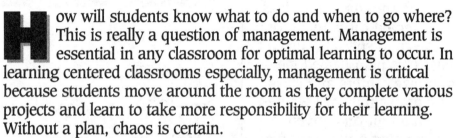
Setting Up
For Success

How will students know what to do and when to go where? This is really a question of management. Management is essential in any classroom for optimal learning to occur. In learning centered classrooms especially, management is critical because students move around the room as they complete various projects and learn to take more responsibility for their learning. Without a plan, chaos is certain.

Having thought through how I intended to use centers, I needed to decide how centers would fit into the entire day. I decided to group students and have them rotate to the various centers in the morning. As with any group activity, there are many ways to combine kids. To start, I was only concerned with making groups equal in size. As I got to know my students, I varied the groups. Mixed ability, like ability, and interest are some of the attributes you might use for grouping. I used each depending on my purposes for the centers.

Mixed ability groups: Use groups in which members perform at different levels on a given task such as working with others to help students learn from one another. This type of grouping enables students to have a greater understanding of others and to develop an increased friendliness toward others, regardless of ability. Mixed ability grouping also equalizes expectations for all learners. In addition, there's no stigma attached to being a member of a given group.

Like ability groups: Use groups in which members perform at the same level on a given task such as ability to comprehend to teach students particular skills or strategies. This type of grouping helps

meet the diverse needs of students in an efficient manner.

Interest groups: Grouping according to like interests enables students within the group to share their areas of expertise. This sharing often leads each group member to refine his or her knowledge related to the interest, thereby becoming an "expert" on the topic.

Center Schedules

Afternoons in my class were reserved for whole group activities and specials such as music. This plan helped me best utilize centers and class time. For example, if I wanted to begin a unit on a given topic by using a video, I often scheduled this activity for the afternoon. On the following day, I had students complete center activities designed to either reinforce or extend the whole group lesson.

Next, of course, comes conveying your plan to students. A simple schedule can show students where they are to be, when they are to be there, and where they are headed next. A schedule that can change with minimal effort and one that is large enough for students to read from several locations in the room is a plus.

Sample Center Schedule	
8:55–9:10	• Opening
9:10–9:35	• First center rotation
9:40–10:10	• Second center rotation
10:15–10:25	• Morning recess
10:30–10:55	• Third center rotation
11:00–11:30	• Fourth center rotation
11:35–12:30	• Lunch/recess break
12:30–1:00	• Group story/independent reading
1:00–1:35	• Mathematics
1:40–1:55	• Afternoon recess
2:00–2:30	• Specials
2:30–3:00	• Whole group activities
3:00–3:15	• Dismissal

This is the schedule for Monday.

Groups	9:10 -9:35	9:40 -10:10		10:30 -10:55	11:00 -11:30
Cyril Jennifer Ray Mikiko	1	2	R E C E S S	3	4
Jay Heidi Ed Denelle Shanita Aaron	2	3		4	1
Matt Leone Julie Michael Vanessa Joe	3	4	R E C E S S	1	2
Paula Josh Jamal Shane Liesl Marisol	4	1		2	3

Day Cards

Center Labels

Name Cards

23

With these needs in mind, the schedule on page 23 shows one way of rotating students through centers. I used different colors of construction paper for the cards (you could also use shapes) and hung the cards from drapery hooks on a schedule board constructed from a 4-by-4-foot piece of cardboard covered with chart paper.

Organizing Your Room

Does the way you organize your classroom now reflect the ways you teach and the ways you want your students to learn? For example, are your desks grouped in pods to promote cooperative learning? Are supplies in easy reach of students to encourage their independence? The way that you set up for learning centers also needs to reflect and facilitate the type of desired learning.

I wanted to create a warm, inviting, cooperative environment with a feeling of coziness. I wanted a bunch of little rooms within the large room, yet I wanted to be able to observe students from any spot in the room. I also wanted to be able to use the room for whole class instruction. How could I create this?

I began by making a map of the classroom. Realizing that I would have to work within their constraints, I penciled in all of the permanent fixtures: doors, windows, electrical outlets, closets, sinks, counters, shelves, and carpet areas.

On another piece of paper, I made a list of the portable furniture in the room. Originally, I had envisioned a desk for each student, arranged in pods toward the middle of the room, with centers around the outer edges of the room. (See sample floor plan, page 25.) With this plan, students would have a place to store their belongings and a place to sit during whole group activities. This was when I realized that there were only seven student desks in the room. Rather than turn my attention to finding more desks, I decided to play around with alternative plans. I made a list of what I would need to create the environment I envisioned:

- five areas, one for each center,

- an area for meeting with the whole class,

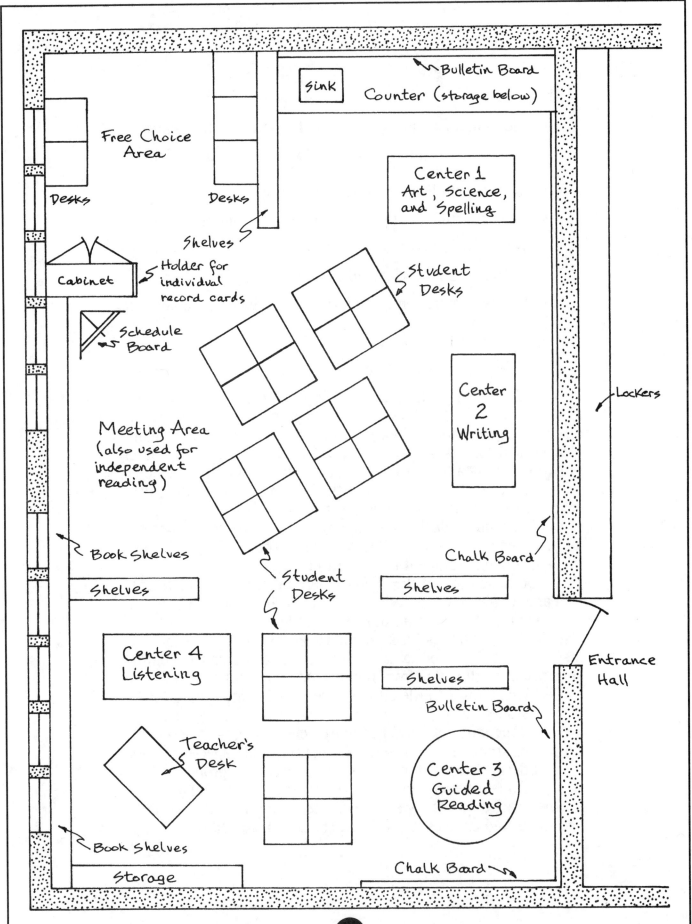

Free Choice Area

Desks

Desks

Sink

Bulletin Board

Counter (storage below)

Center 1
Art, Science, and Spelling

Shelves

Holder for individual record cards

Cabinet

Schedule Board

Student Desks

Center 2 Writing

Lockers

Meeting Area (also used for independent reading)

Book Shelves

Shelves

Student Desks

Chalk Board

Shelves

Entrance Hall

Center 4 Listening

Shelves

Bulletin Board

Teacher's Desk

Center 3 Guided Reading

Book Shelves

Storage

Chalk Board

- quiet and noisy areas spaced as far apart as possible,

- traffic patterns allowing easy flow from one area of the room to the next,
- places for students to store their things,

- places for students to sit during whole group activities,

- display areas for student creations,

- bookshelves for a classroom library,

- shelves to store center materials and create the illusion of little rooms,
- a schedule board, and

- an area to store class supplies and materials.

After much plotting and erasing, my plan emerged. A close look reveals that I was able to incorporate everything I had on my list. (See sample floor plan #2, page 27.) I was especially pleased with the traffic pattern. Students could enter each center in two ways, by a front and back door, if you will. Thus, when one group was entering one way, the previous group exited the other way. Students were able to rotate clockwise. The problem of too few student desks challenged me to reconsider my view of a classroom and inspired a floor plan that successfully reflected the learning environment I wanted to create.

Because none of the shelves were taller than three feet, I was able to observe the various centers without difficulty and at the same time maintain an illusion of little rooms. Center tables also doubled as places for students to sit during whole group instruction. If I wanted to have all students focus on the board, I simply moved the table from the instructional center out of its corner. This required little effort. I used the bulletin boards to display student work and to post directions for the centers. I arranged the student desks in the free choice center, reserving a couple for students who needed a quiet, separate space at times.

I decided to use bins (cubbies) to solve the problem of storing student belongings. I visited the local ice-cream parlor for the next couple of days and collected containers that would become round cubbies. Once I had enough, I stapled them

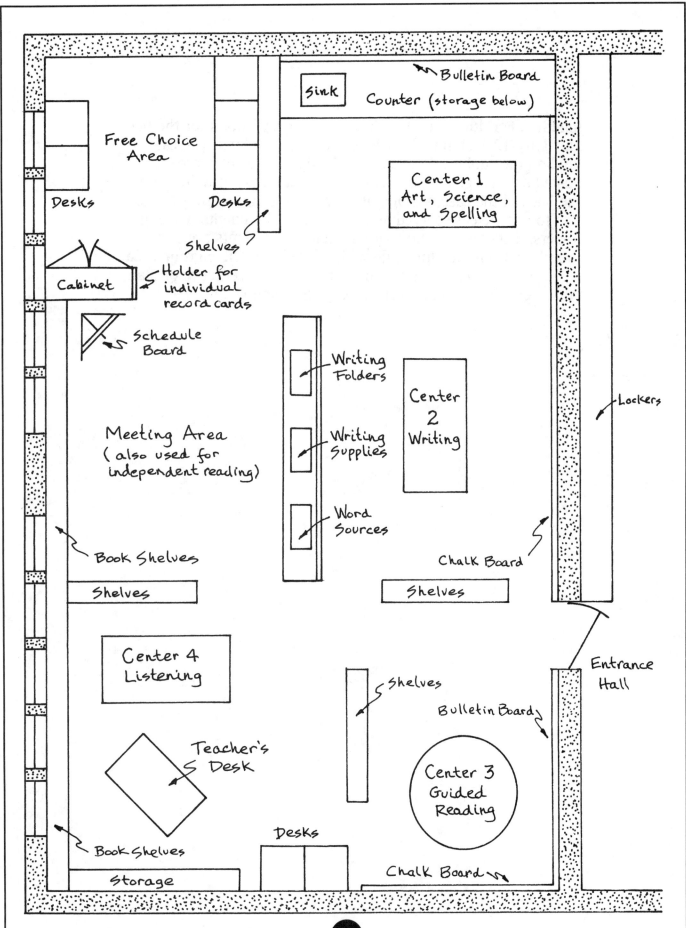

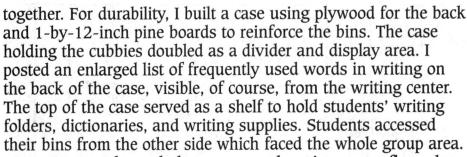

together. For durability, I built a case using plywood for the back and 1-by-12-inch pine boards to reinforce the bins. The case holding the cubbies doubled as a divider and display area. I posted an enlarged list of frequently used words in writing on the back of the case, visible, of course, from the writing center. The top of the case served as a shelf to hold students' writing folders, dictionaries, and writing supplies. Students accessed their bins from the other side which faced the whole group area.

As you plot and plan your own learning center floor plan, you might find the checklist on page 29 helpful.

Learning Center Checklist

Work spaces:
_____ space for each center planned
_____ student desks (if applicable)
_____ quiet work space
_____ "noisy" work area
_____ whole group activity area

Storage spaces:
_____ center activities file cabinet (copy paper boxes work well, too)
_____ individual student storage areas
_____ class supplies storage spaces
_____ shelves for each planned center
_____ bookshelves

Display spaces:
_____ class schedule
_____ student rotation schedule board
_____ student work displays
_____ center directions

Traffic patterns:
_____ easy flow from one center to the next
_____ an enter and exit option for each center

Permanent fixtures:
_____ door
_____ electrical outlets (keep in mind when locating listening center)
_____ sink (place art center nearby)
_____ shelves (can help create illusion of separate rooms)
_____ carpeted areas (locate large group area here)

Managing Materials

Although I now teach at the university, I find myself continuing to add to my learning center collections. Not long ago, for example, I was at a garage sale where I noticed some ice cube trays shaped like dinosaurs. "Perfect for my dinosaur center" I told myself as I picked them up. My wife was in a state of disbelief. "Why are you getting those? You don't teach first grade anymore." "I know," I countered, "but these are a perfect for a dinosaur center."

And so the collecting, once started, continues. To assist in storing, organizing, and accessing your own treasure-chest of materials and activities, try these tips:

Storing supplies: I found cardboard file boxes, stored on shelves with labels facing out, to be a huge help. At the start of a new center, label a box with the name of the center. Use it to store materials such as books, printed directions, other center displays, and activity planning sheets. To keep track of materials that are too large for the boxes (such as, posters and commercially prepared board games), make a list of materials and where they are stored (closets, shelves, etc.) and place this record in the box.

This system enabled me to locate materials with ease. It also enabled me to add to the centers even when I wasn't using them (as with my dinosaur ice cube trays). You'll want to have a couple of extra boxes on hand for materials you come across that you want to use in the future.

Easy access to activities: As you develop student activities for your centers (and discover ways to use existing materials), you'll want to have a system in place for filing. I coded activities for various centers (labeling them with numbers) and, if appropriate,

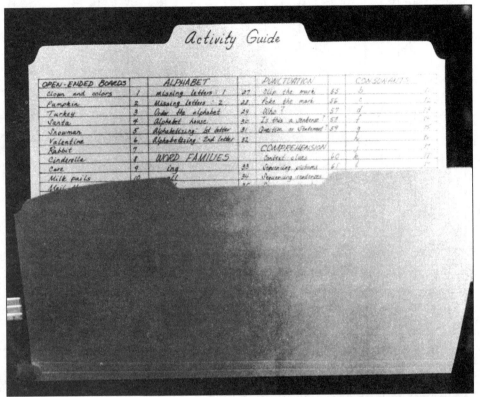

Activity Guide

OPEN-ENDED BOARDS		ALPHABET		PUNCTUATION		CONSONANTS	
Clown and colors	1	Missing letters : 1	27	Slip the mark	55	b	
Pumpkin	2	Missing letters : 2	28	Poke the mark	56	c	
Turkey	3	Order the alphabet	29	Who ?	57	d	
Santa	4	Alphabet house	30	Is this a sentence ?	58	f	
Snowman	5	Alphabetizing : 1st letter	31	Question or Statement ?	59	g	
Valentine	6	Alphabetizing : 2nd letter	32			h	
Rabbit	7			COMPREHENSION		j	
Cinderella	8	WORD FAMILIES		Context clues	60	k	
Cars	9	ing	33	Sequencing pictures	61	l	
Milk pails	10	all	34	Sequencing sentences			

sequenced them in order of complexity. I then constructed activity guides from file folders, and listed each center's activities and code numbers. (See sample activity guide page 32.)

These guides not only let you easily see what you already have to teach certain skills and concepts, they also let you find them quickly in your files (by matching numbers). I filed the guides in the front of the filing cabinet or box where I stored the activities.

Organizing materials at the centers: If you're using activities for an entire group, put them in a box, place the box in the center, and have students complete them as they rotate through. If you want to have specific children complete certain activities, use your guide to pull the appropriate activities, and place them in the center with a chart listing students' names and the activity(ies) each needs to complete.

OPEN-ENDED BOARDS

Activity	#
Clown and colors	1
Pumpkin	2
Turkey	3
Santa	4
Snowman	5
Valentine	6
Rabbit	7
Cinderella	8
Cave	9
Milk Pails	10
Mail the letter	11
Star journey	12
Lead me home	13
Buzz to the honey	14
Ladybug	15
Pitch a winner	16
Bingo cards	17
Wipe off cards	18

CONTRACTIONS

Activity	#
're and 've	19
's	20
n't	21
'm and 'll	22
all contractions	23

PREFIXES

Activity	#
un	24
re	25
pre	26

ALPHABET

Activity	#
Missing letters: 1	27
Missing letters: 2	28
Order the alphabet	29
Alphabet house	30
Alphabetizing 1st letter	31
Alphabetizing 2nd letter	32

WORD FAMILIES

ing
all
ill
ell
ig
ake
at
an
it
et
in
op
ot
ug
ame
ine
ight
at, an, it, ill
ake, an, et, ell (review)
dominoes (review)
tray puzzle
cards for sorting

PUNCTUATION

Activity	#
Clip the mark	55
Poke the mark	56
Who?	57
Is this a sentence?	58
Question or Statement?	59

COMPREHENSION

Activity	#
Context clues	60
Sequencing pictures	61
Sequencing sentences	62
Sequencing events	63
Get the facts	64
Fact or opinion?	65
Details, details	66
Main idea	67
Draw a conclusion	68
Infer!	69
Make a prediction	70
Follow the directions	71

VOCABULARY

Activity	#
Antonyms	72
Synonyms	73
Homonyms	74
Multiple meanings	75
Compound words	76
Listening for syllables	77
How many syllables?	78
Feed the horses	79
Crosswords	80

CONSONANTS

Letter	#
b	81
c	82
d	83
f	84
g	85
h	86
j	87
k	88
l	89
m	90
n	91
p	92
q	93
r	94
s	95
t	96
v	97
w	98
x	99
y	100
z	101

CONSONANT BLENDS

Blend	#
fl	102
bl	103
cl	104
tr	105
gr	106
cr	107
br	108

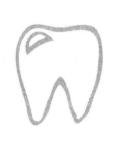

CHAPTER 3
Assessment Options

As with any effective instruction, there must be a definite purpose for a given center activity. In fact, I've found that an effective learning center is one in which an overall purpose has been established with learners in mind. When you begin planning with a purpose, you also lay the foundation for meaningful assessment. By asking and answering the question "What do I want students to accomplish?" you give direction to the activity and establish a framework for assessment.

For example, in planning a writing center activity, you might want children to write or dictate stories about something they are experts at. By establishing a purpose, rather than simply asking students to write stories, you provide a focus for evaluation. (Did the child identify and write about an area of expertise, for example, taking care of a pet, playing baseball, or making pictures?) Some guidelines for this process follow.

1. Think about your general purpose. Will the center introduce, reinforce, or extend a given learning?

2. Formulate a specific objective. Exactly what do you want students to do at the center?

3. Decide how many activities you will include. To guide selection, you might consider the following options:

• Place one activity at the center that all students will complete. This option is appropriate when the purpose of the center is to reinforce concepts to which all students have been exposed. It's also useful when the purpose is to introduce all students to an upcoming unit of study, such as the five senses.

• Place more than one activity related to the purpose and

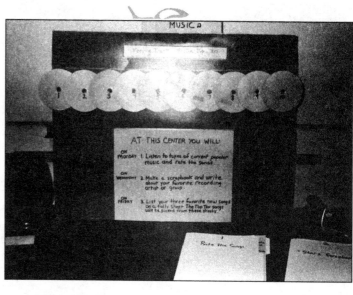

objective at the center and have students choose one to complete. For example, if the objective of the center is to help students learn about compound words, students can make word puzzles using strips of construction paper on which they write compound words and cut them apart at the appropriate places. They can also create word puzzles and locate compound words in a section of the newspaper. Using this option also helps reinforce students' decision-making skills.

• Place several activities at the center and assign certain activities for specific students or groups. When students rotate to the center, they complete those activities labeled with their names. This option allows for mixed ability grouping while at the same time providing for individual differences.

4. Decide how many content areas you want to incorporate. Most often I integrated one of the language arts with at least one other content area such as science. By providing printed instructions, you can tie reading in at every center. Not only do these directions familiarize students with environmental print, they also facilitate student independence.

5. Select materials for use at each center. One word really helped me when considering materials: **variety**! Games, filmstrips, books, tape recorders, manipulatives, and writing and art supplies, are just a few materials for stocking centers. Of course, they need to be geared toward

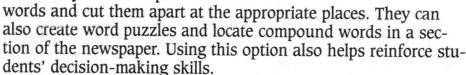

the purpose of the centers and selected with students in mind. Clearly, the materials are more than worksheets sprinkled around the room at centers.

Center activity planning sheet:
I constructed a center activity planning sheet to record all of my initial decisions about a center: from general purpose to student directions. These planning sheets served as checklists as I went about setting up specific activities within the centers. They also served as handy tools to guide assessment. (Sample on page 36.)

CENTER ACTIVITY PLANNING SHEET

Title: _____

Content area(s): _____

Purpose: Introduce   Reinforce   Extend

Objective(s): _____

_____

_____

Materials:

STUDENT DIRECTIONS

Here's what you'll need:

Here's what you do:

Keeping Track

What's the best way to keep track of what students accomplish? When I first attempted to answer this question, I found that there were many ways to keep records. Rather than search for one right way, I chose and created systems that would best suit my purposes for using centers. I also had students keep as many of the records as possible for I felt that doing so would help them develop more responsibility for their own learning.

Weekly group folder: The weekly group folder was one device I created for my own use. I developed a cover sheet (see page 38) and affixed it to the cover of a folder for each group. If you have groups that will be unchanged for a period of time, you might make a master cover sheet. Each day, I listed students' names on the appropriate space on this cover sheet. As students completed each center, I made a quick check to see if each member had attempted the center. If so, I placed a check next to the child's name. Any papers completed at the centers went into the folder. You can use an asterisk to represent the group leader who was responsible for carrying the folder from one center to the next.

I used this system when students rotated as groups (based on the schedule shown on page 23.) This approach was effective in helping me organize my records and in accomplishing my main goals for using centers—teaching students how to work with others and how to work together as a team. Students knew exactly what had to be completed, when it had to be completed, and how it needed to be completed. Clearly, it was not the free for all sometimes conjured up of children running everywhere and anywhere, completing activities in a haphazard manner. Instead, this system provided students freedom within a specified structure.

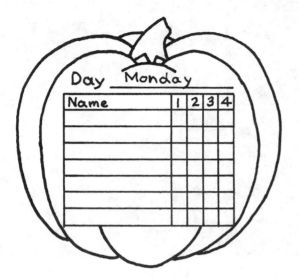

Day Monday					
Name		1	2	3	4

Day Tuesday					
Name		1	2	3	4

Day Wednesday					
Name		1	2	3	4

Day Thursday					
Name		1	2	3	4

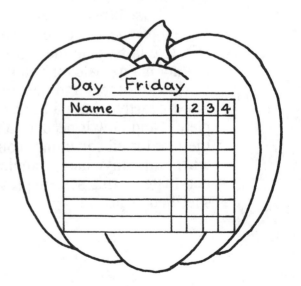

Day Friday					
Name		1	2	3	4

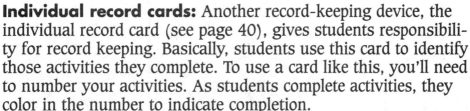

Individual record cards: Another record-keeping device, the individual record card (see page 40), gives students responsibility for record keeping. Basically, students use this card to identify those activities they complete. To use a card like this, you'll need to number your activities. As students complete activities, they color in the number to indicate completion.

What I like about this form is that it's generic. Since my activities were all numbered to begin with, all I had to do was change the numbers on the sheet to correspond to the particular activities at the centers. As students became more comfortable with making choices, I could add additional activities from which to choose. I started with a choice of six activities and gradually built up to sixteen. Another option is to create a sheet with four (or the number of centers) cards, each identifying the activities in those centers for the day or week.

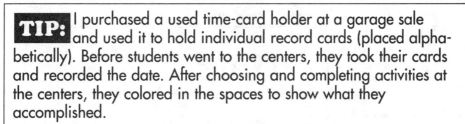

TIP: I purchased a used time-card holder at a garage sale and used it to hold individual record cards (placed alphabetically). Before students went to the centers, they took their cards and recorded the date. After choosing and completing activities at the centers, they colored in the spaces to show what they accomplished.

Variations on Record-Keeping

The center activity planning sheet, weekly group folder, and individual record cards provide a general framework for keeping track of students' center work. However, you can create and use others to meet additional needs. For example, sometimes I wanted to have students keep track of the *variety* of activities they completed on one topic. For a senses center, I created a special form for students to complete which I stapled to their individual folders. Students then checked off each item they completed. (See My Five Senses, page 41.) Again, students placed completed work in the folders which they kept in a file box at the center. When the unit was complete, students could take their folders home to share with families.

Name

(1) (2)

(3) (4)

(5) (6)

Name

(1) (2) (3) (4)

(5) (6) (7) (8)

(9) (10) (11) (12)

(13) (14) (15) (16)

Tasting   Seeing   Hearing

My **5** Senses

Touching

Smelling

Name: _____

I did the "Using Your Senes" center.	☐
I wrote a story about my senses.	☐
I listened to the tape and watched the filmstrip "Look How You See".	☐
I labeled and wrote about my eyes.	☐
I found the hidden pictures.	☐
I listened to the tape and watched the filmstrip "Here Is Your Ear".	☐
I labeled the parts of my ear.	☐
I listened to the tape and watched the filmstrip "Watch How Your Nose Knows".	☐
I made a smell collage.	☐
I listened to the tape and watched the filmstrip "Your Tasting Tongue".	☐
I made a list of things I taste.	☐
I made a Mr. Tasty.	☐
I listened to the tape and watched the filmstrip "Feel of Your Skin".	☐
I wrote about things I touch.	☐
I made a Touching Words Mobile.	☐
I read the book My Five Senses.	☐

Evaluating Students' Work

When thinking about evaluation, you might want to consider the following components.

1. Student use

For example: Did they stay on task? Did they return materials to the proper place? Did they work cooperatively? Did they show that they were able to work independently?

2. Actual products (student work)

If applicable: Just how well was the product completed? Was it accurate? Did it show that the student accomplished the established purpose?

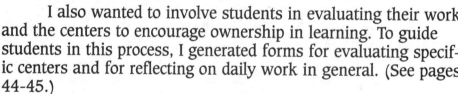

3. The actual center

In looking at the centers themselves: Were the directions clearly stated? Were there enough materials? Did the center address different learning styles?

To address these questions, I constructed a generic form (see page 43) that enabled me to evaluate specific attributes. You can use this evaluation form as you observe students working—both to assess their progress and to evaluate specific aspects of the centers themselves.

I also wanted to involve students in evaluating their work and the centers to encourage ownership in learning. To guide students in this process, I generated forms for evaluating specific centers and for reflecting on daily work in general. (See pages 44-45.)

LEARNING CENTER EVALUATION

Evaluation Attributes

Name:

Listener's Evaluation

Your name _____

Name of story _____

I liked the story: (circle one)

   a lot   some   not much

One part I liked was _____

_____

_____

or

One part I didn't like was

_____

_____

Would you tell a friend to
   listen to this story ?
            (circle one)

         Yes No

Daily Evaluation

Name _____

Week of _____

	M	T	W	Th	F
I followed directions.					
I completed all activities.					
I completed work neatly.					
I listened.					
I cooperated with my group.					

Rating scale:

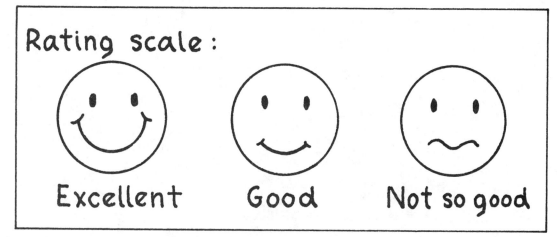

Excellent   Good   Not so good

One goal I have for myself:

_____

_____

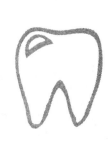

PART TWO

KEEPING THEM GOING!

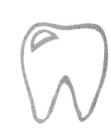

CHAPTER 4
THE FIRST WEEK

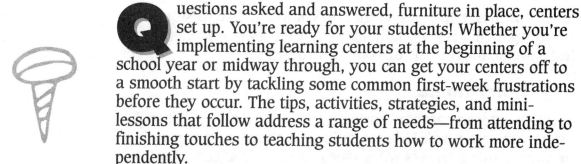

Questions asked and answered, furniture in place, centers set up. You're ready for your students! Whether you're implementing learning centers at the beginning of a school year or midway through, you can get your centers off to a smooth start by tackling some common first-week frustrations before they occur. The tips, activities, strategies, and mini-lessons that follow address a range of needs—from attending to finishing touches to teaching students how to work more independently.

Before Students Arrive

Get ready for your first day with learning centers by taking a trial run yourself. The following checklist can help you make sure your room is ready to go.

_____ Color-coded name tags

I began by dividing the class into four groups, equal in size and balanced in gender. I made name tags using four colors, one for each group. If you're implementing centers at the start of the school year, you can place these name tags on the door along with a welcome sign.

_____ First-day activities

I selected activities for the four centers, choosing activities that students would be able to complete without my assistance and those that would help students get to know one another. These

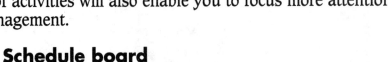

types of activities will also enable you to focus more attention on management.

_____ Schedule board

I wanted students to begin using a schedule board (see page 23) from day one. To reinforce the groupings, match schedule board card colors to the color-coded name tags.

_____ Tote trays

Label students' tote trays so that they know where to store their belongings. This is especially important if separate student desks are no longer part of your class design.

_____ Letter home

I wrote a letter to parents sharing my view of teaching, describing how the room would be organized this year, and explaining the way learning centers work (see page 51). You can adapt the letter for the time of year you start using centers and to reflect your own way of teaching. Letters like these encourage parents to be informed and involved from the beginning—an important factor in students' success.

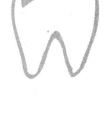

Sample Letter to Parents

Dear _____,

 Welcome to second grade! My name is Michael Opitz and I am writing you this letter to tell you a little bit about your child's classroom this year.

 I believe that all children can and want to learn. As a teacher, my main goal is to help your child learn to be an independent, lifelong learner. To reach this goal, I will meet your child from where he/she is at and guide him/her as far as possible, planning very carefully so that your child can feel challenged without unnecessary frustration. Teaching children that their best efforts are essential when completing a task is another goal. I want your child to develop and maintain an "I can and will try" attitude. I feel this attitude enables success.

 To accomplish my goals, I use learning centers. Your child will be completing activities and projects in centers around the room, each designed to focus on a different area, such as writing and listening. In addition to teaching academics, learning centers provide opportunities for children to learn other important skills, such as responsibility, decision-making, and self-evaluation.

 Your question may well be "Does this approach work?" My answer is "Yes!" Learning centers are more than an engaging way to teach and learn. By offering a variety of activities that draw on different strengths, learning centers help give all students a chance to learn in a way that best suits them.

 I am constantly perfecting the centers as I continue to grow. I welcome any suggestions, help, and materials you would like to offer as you support your child's learning experience. I'm looking forward to meeting you at open house. Your child will be able to explain our learning centers to you and I will be happy to answer any questions you have.

 It's my pleasure to work with your child. I'm looking forward to a year filled with learning!

Sincerely,
Michael F. Opitz

A Five-Day Plan

This day-by-day plan walks you through your first week—from welcoming students to recognizing and addressing special needs. You can easily adapt many of the suggestions. For example, you might make name tags for younger students but let older students design name tags that represent their groups.

Day 1: Welcome students to their new learning environment, giving each a color-coded name tag. Once all students have arrived, hold a group meeting in the meeting area. Provide a brief overview of how the classroom is set up and how they will be working.

I purposely kept this overview brief because past experience has taught me that students learn best by doing. Students can learn more about the approach by actually working at the centers the first day. In addition to the usual events of the day, then, my goals for this first day of learning centers were geared toward management: helping students become familiar with their groups, with rotating from center to center, with reading the schedule, and so on.

First-Day Grouping Game

Use students' color-coded name tags for a get-to-know-your-groups game. Begin by explaining: "Some of you belong together. I can tell by looking at your name tags. See if you can figure out the other classmates who belong to you by looking at their name tags and sit together."

Once in groups, use the schedule chart to reinforce the groups: "Let's take a look at our schedule. It also tells which students go together today." Invite students to read the chart to find out where they go first. Dismiss groups one by one to their first center.

Center Signals

Like any new skill, students need practice rotating from center to center with a minimum of disruption. One way to help is to develop and practice a system of signals. For example, you might clap a certain rhythm or play/sing a strand of music to let

students know they need to stop and listen. At this time, you could let students know they have five more minutes at the center, that it's time to rotate, and so on. Alternately, you might devise separate signals to represent set messages. Three claps might mean students have three minutes left to work at a center. A toot on a horn might signal it's time to clean up, and so on.

Rules and Expectations

When students are able to read and follow the schedule, many problems can be avoided. I constantly referred to the schedule to reinforce the importance of it and being able to do what it said.

I also established some initial rules and expectations for working at centers, keeping this list to a minimum, though, because I wanted students to see the meaning behind each stated expectation. They would best be able to see this meaning if the expectation evolved out of something that actually happened. For example, if the noise level is too high on a given day, this would be a good time to state expectations about proper noise level.

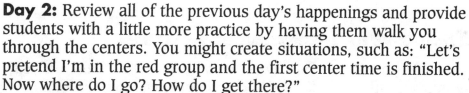

Day 2: Review all of the previous day's happenings and provide students with a little more practice by having them walk you through the centers. You might create situations, such as: "Let's pretend I'm in the red group and the first center time is finished. Now where do I go? How do I get there?"

Next introduce the group folder and demonstrate how it works (see page 37). Introduce each center activity by reading the directions with students and demonstrating how to complete the center. I had students sit and stand around each center as I explained and demonstrated the activities. Once you've explained all of the centers, students can complete them in turn, according to the day's schedule, while you watch and work with students, giving help where needed.

From the start, you'll get to know your students better and gain valuable information for evaluation: How does each go about completing activities? How do students appear to get along with other group members? Introduce students to self-

evaluation by having them complete a review of the day (see Daily Evaluation, page 45).

Days 3 and 4: Again, review what's been introduced to date. Explain and demonstrate new center activities. Then have students complete each, following established procedures. As you observe students working, you can facilitate the process by reminding them where to look for specific materials or assisting them in rereading directions.

Day 5: The fifth day repeats the procedures of days three and four. However, on this day, you might try to stay in one center only if you plan on concentrating your attention on different areas, different days. If, for example, you're introducing a new skill at one center, and reinforcing skills at others, you might choose to spend most of your time assisting at this particular center. You can let students know by saying something like: "Today when you complete centers, you'll notice that I will be at the reading center most of the morning. I want to see if you can complete the rest of your centers without any help from me today. I think you'll do well. . ."

Encouraging Independent Learners

As you observe students at the centers, you'll undoubtedly notice some areas of need. Do students need help becoming more independent in their center work? Are there materials and equipment that students are unfamiliar with? Do students demonstrate appropriate behaviors when completing their center work? You can focus on specific topics such as these by presenting 10-minute mini-lessons.

I discovered that these lessons prevented much frustration for both the students and myself. For example, if I presented a lesson showing students how to use new materials, I was less likely to be interrupted when working with individuals or groups. Fewer interruptions meant less frustration for me. Students were less frustrated because they knew how to use the materials and what to do if a malfunction occurred.

A starter list of topics, as well as three fully developed sample mini-lessons, follows. As you implement your centers and watch your students work, you might add your own topics. When trying to decide if a topic warrants a mini-lesson, ask yourself, "Is this lesson essential in order for students to be successful, independent learners?" If yes, add the topic to your list. Regardless of the topic, I found that planning lessons that included the following four parts helped students better understand the lesson:

1. A focus, stating the purpose for the lesson.

2. An explanation, providing students with information related to the purpose.

3. Role playing, giving students opportunities for practice.

4. Direct application, letting students use the skill or information when completing the centers.

Sample Mini-Lesson 1: Caring for Materials

Focus: caring for materials
Explanation: "Yesterday I noticed that all of you were doing an excellent job of completing center activities on time. I also noticed that you knew exactly where to get your materials for completing your activities. Today I want to show you how to care for the materials.

15 Mini-Lesson Topics

- rotating from center to center
- reading the schedule board
- recognizing clean-up (and other) signals
- storing finished products
- using appropriate volume
- being a good group leader
- being a good group member
- locating help
- signalling the teacher without being disruptive
- handling a problem (e.g., paint spills, pencil breaks)
- handling free time
- using a tape recorder
- keeping records
- caring for materials

Your Own Mini-Lesson Topics:
- _____
- _____
- _____
- _____
- _____

The first thing you need to remember is to read the directions for the center and to notice where materials are stored. Then you take the materials you need to complete the activity. Before you leave, though, you must leave the center exactly as you found it—cleaned up with materials in the proper place."

> **TIP:** You might list basic points on chart paper and post for easy reference as students role play during this lesson and as they work in the centers.

Role play: Let's do some role playing. I'll be the student and I'll use the center. You watch me and see if I do what I just told you to do." Go to the center and follow all directions except for the last one, putting materials away. Then turn to students and say, "I'm finished! I guess I'll go to the next center. May I go?"

If students respond, "No!" invite them to explain what you need to do. (Encourage them to indicate that you need to put materials in their proper places.) Follow their directions, then say, "Now may I leave?"

Direct application: Close the lesson by asking students to review the procedure for caring for materials. Explain that you'll be paying special attention to this today. Remind group leaders to make sure that each group member cares for materials when completing centers.

Sample Mini-Lesson 2: Rotating to Centers

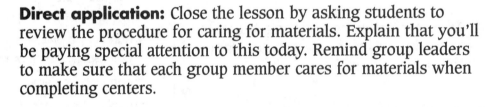

Focus: rotating from center to center

Explanation: Ask students to describe rules they see their parents or the bus driver following when they drive. Explain, for example: "When you ride in the car with your parents, you've probably noticed that they go down the street on a certain side and that they know when to stop and go. Their knowing these things helps you to get from one place to the other safely. Well, our classroom is the same way. There is a certain way to go to centers and a certain way to leave. This is what I want to show

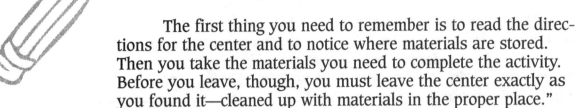

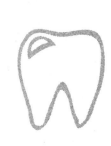

you today." Walk students through the traffic pattern
you have selected for your centers (for example, clockwise).

> **TIP:** You might construct and post Enter and Exit signs
> as a visual aid.

Role play: Stand by Center 1 and say, "I'm at Center 1 and it's
time for me to move to Center 2. Which way do I go?" Have students talk you through the directions. Repeat this procedure for
all centers. Then have four students, one at each center, go
through the process. Say: "These people need to move to their
next center. Let's watch and see if they move in the right direction." Have students rotate. Now ask the class if they moved in
the right direction. Continue until the four students are back at
their original centers.

Direct application: As students begin their center rotations,
remind them that to avoid traffic jams, they need to move in the
right direction.

Sample Mini-Lesson 3: Recognizing Signals

Focus: signals for cleaning up and moving to the next center (or
any other activity as indicated)

Explanation: "We need to have a secret code that will let you
know that I need your attention. Let's try this one. When you are
working at your center and you hear me toot this horn (or clap
this rhythm or play this tune, etc.), you need to stop what you
are doing and get ready to listen to an important announcement.
This way you won't miss out on anything! Let's try it!

> **TIP:** Signals like "lights out" may be so familiar to students
> that they may not respond as well as you'd like. For
> variety and added fun, try something new or unusual.

Role play: Walk over to a center and pretend to be completing
an activity. Have a student give the signal and instruct others to

watch what you do. When the signal is given, stop what you are doing, then ask, "Did I do the right thing?" Students should respond "Yes!" Next, choose six students to go to a center and pretend to complete an activity. Have the rest of the students watch what happens when you give the signal. Ask, "What happened?" (Did all six remember to stop what they were doing?)

Direct application: Say: "Today I'm going to give you a lot of practice with this signal as you complete your centers. You never know when I might give the signal. Let's see if you can remember every time! I bet you can."

CHAPTER 5

LEARNING CENTERS YOU CAN USE

I've found that one of the most effective ways to teach is to organize learning around student interests whenever possible and around what is actually happening during a given month. Instead of pretending that Halloween doesn't exist, for example, October might be a good time to introduce students to the part of your curriculum that deals with nocturnal animals such as bats, cats, and owls.

You can use these topics as springboards to creating themed centers that stimulate student interest and learning. Topic bursts allow you to keep the basic structure of the centers intact while changing content to reflect interests and timely topics.

You can easily adapt the topic-burst approach according to how you decide to use centers. If you use centers to **append** the curriculum, the centers would be supplemental; some students would complete them whereas others would not. If you use centers to **extend**, all students would complete the centers with a given time frame. If you use centers to **organize and deliver** your curriculum, students would rotate to the various centers and actually learn the content through the centers.

Following are three sample topic bursts and an alphabet of ideas. Each sample burst shows

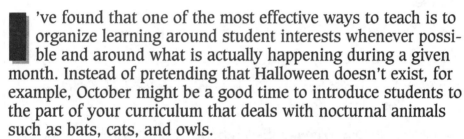

September:	Apples
October:	Pumpkins
November:	Food groups
December:	Community helpers (Post office workers)
January:	Teeth
February:	Friendship
March:	Fitness (National Nutrition Month)
April:	Eggs
May:	Animals (Be Kind to Animals Week)
June:	Rivers (National Rivers

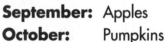

how a topic is integrated into the centers with activities that address specific objectives of the curriculum.

TIP: If you organize learning centers by themes, you can help children make reading connections by incorporating related books at the centers. Helpful resources for locating books by topic (as well as by author and illustrator) include:

A to Zoo: Subject Access to Children's Picture Books by Carolyn W. Lima and John A. Lima (Bowker)

Best Books for Children by John T. Gillespie and Corinne J. Naden (Bowker)

Books Kids Will Sit Still For by Judy Freeman (Bowker)

Eyeopeners! by Beverly Kobrin (Penguin)

The New York Times Parent's Guide to the Best Books for Children by Eden Ross Lipson (Random House)

Portraying Persons With Disabilities by Joan Brest Friedberg, June B. Mullins, and Adelaide Weir Sukiennik (Bowker)

Center 1: Spelling

Objective:
to learn to spell words associated with teeth.

Activity:
*1. Post a list of words associated with teeth on a tooth-shaped chart.
2. Have students choose at least three words to learn to spell. You might offer tooth-shaped paper for completing this activity.

* sample words: incisor, root, molar, cavity, toothbrush, floss, toothpaste

Center 2: Writing

Objective:
to write about a personal experience.

Activity:
Instruct students to write about a time when they lost a tooth. Students can use tooth-shaped paper for writing final drafts then bind to make books.

Topic: Teeth

Center 3: Reading

Objective:
to recall information stated in the text.

Activity:
Read <u>Little Rabbit's Lost Tooth</u>.
Have students retell the story orally.

Center 4: Listening

Objective:
to increase listening comprehension.

Activity:
Have students listen to <u>One Morning in Maine</u> and complete a listening evaluation.

Center 1: Spelling

Objective:
to learn to spell names of animals that hatch from eggs.

Activity:
Put names of animals that hatch from eggs on word strips. Cut each apart and put each into a plastic egg. Have students sequence letters in correct order.

Possible words: duck, snake, alligator, turtle, ostrich, chicken, fish, frog, snail, dinosaur.

Center 2: Writing

Objective:
to sequence phrases into meaningful sentences.

Activity:
Provide students with three baskets, each filled with phrases written on paper egg shapes. Instruct them to take a phrase from each basket and put them into an order that makes sense.

Topic: Eggs

Center 3: Reading

Objective:
to recall information stated in text.

Activity:
1. Read and discuss Chickens Aren't the Only Ones.
2. Brainstorm with students all of the animals that come from eggs. Write their responses on a chart shaped like an egg.

Center 4: Listening

Objective:
to increase literal listening.

Activity:
Have students listen to Little Chicks Story. Ask them to draw pictures showing what happened first, second, and so on.

Center 1 : Spelling

Objective:
to spell words located within one large word.

Activity:
Have students see how many words they can spell using the letters in the word _friendship_.

Center 2 : Writing

Objective:
to learn how to write a friendly letter.

Activity:
After showing students the parts that make up a friendly letter, have have them use this format to write a letter to a friend.

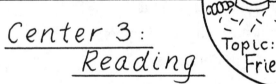

Topic: Friendship

Center 3 : Reading

Objective:
to improve ability to make inferences.

Activity:
Have students read _Move Over, Twerp_. Discuss if Jeffrey and the others become friends.

Center 4 : Listening

Objective:
to increase listening comprehension.

Activity:
Have students listen to _My Friend Jacob_ and complete a listening evaluation.

AN ALPHABET OF IDEAS

A art, alphabetizing, animals

B blocks, books, bilingual

C cooking, colors, computer

D dinosaurs, drama, discovery

E ecology, explorers, eggs

F five senses, food groups, friendship

G graphs, geometry, games

H health, hobbies, holidays

I ice, inventions, illustrations

J journey, jokes, junk

K kites, karate, kits

L listening, literature, letter writing

M monsters, magnets, measurement

N newspaper, nocturnal animals, numbers

O oral reading, origami, outlining

P puppets, plants, poetry

Q quirks, quotes, questions

R rhyming, reading, riddles

S spelling, sports, sequence

T teeth, tall tales, toys

U unicorns, urchins, unsung heroes

V vocabulary, vultures, viewing

W writing, whales, wizard

X x-ray, extra special, xylophone

Y you, yard, year

Z zoo, zoology, zones

Sample Center Activities

I use Center Activity Planning Sheets to develop and organize my centers (see page 66-79). These forms are time-savers, too. Instead of starting from scratch from year to year, you can use the filing system described in Chapter 2 and have activities that address certain needs and interests at your fingertips.

Following are sample activity plans for a four-center approach that integrates language arts throughout the curriculum (reading, writing, listening, spelling). The first four are center activities I used in conjunction with a five senses unit. Note that these center activities correspond to the floor plan shown on page 27 and the record form shown on page 38.

The next three center activities are more general. By simply selecting appropriate materials, such as children's literature, you can adapt them to support a particular content area. For example, you can use "Listen to a Story" to teach science or social studies by selecting book titles that introduce, extend, or reinforce given concepts. Each activity is designed to integrate one or more of the language arts.

The remaining six activities are suitable for more subject-specific centers, such as language arts, social studies, art, mathematics, and science. Again, because language arts is incorporated into each, the activities work as well at a writing or reading center as they do at a science or math center.

Think Multiculturally

Almost every learning center theme has the potential to provide children with a multicultural experience. For example, if you turn your science center into a Five Senses Exploratorium, you could provide students with foods, fabrics, and musical instruments from other cultures. If you turn your social studies center into an Endangered Animal Sanctuary, you might display pictures and stuffed animals representing endangered animals from around the world.

CENTER ACTIVITY PLANNING SHEET

Title: All About Senses

Content area(s): Health (five senses) and
Language Arts (reading)

Purpose: (Introduce)   (Reinforce)   Extend

Objective(s): to demonstrate comprehension
of the five senses
to practice word identification

Materials:

- books – <u>My Five Senses</u> by aliki
- pencils
- crayons
- white ditto paper

STUDENT DIRECTIONS

Here's what you'll need:

- a book
- a pencil
- crayons
- white paper

Here's what you do:

1. Silently, read the book.
2. Take one paper.
3. Fold it into six parts.

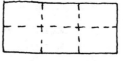

4. Write one sense word in each box.

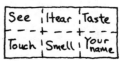

| See | Hear | Taste |
| Touch | Smell | Your name |

5. Draw or write one thing the boy used each sense for.
6. Write your name in the last box.
7. Color your pictures.

66

CENTER ACTIVITY PLANNING SHEET

Title: Spell Sense Words

Content area(s): Health (five senses) and
Language Arts (spelling)

Purpose: (Introduce)　　(Reinforce)　　(Extend)

Objective(s): to learn to spell words associated
with the five senses

Materials:

- five posters, each listing words associated with one of the five senses.
- spelling list forms
- pencils
- scissors

STUDENT DIRECTIONS

Here's what you'll need:

- a pencil
- scissors
- a spelling list form

Here's what you do:

1. Choose two words from each sense that you would like to learn to spell.
2. Copy each word on the spelling list form two times - once on the <u>Take Home List</u> side and once on the <u>School List</u> side.
3. Write your name and date at the top of both lists.
4. Cut the form in half up the middle.
5. Put the <u>Take Home List</u> in your mailbox.
6. Put the <u>School List</u> in your group folder.

Name _____   Name _____

Date _____   Date _____

Take Home List   ## School List

1.

2.

3.

4.

5.

6.

7.

8.

9.

10.

CENTER ACTIVITY PLANNING SHEET

Title: Write a Senses Story

Content area(s): Health (five senses) and

Language Arts (writing)

Purpose: (Introduce)   (Reinforce)   Extend

Objective(s): to introduce the five senses

to practice writing skills

Materials:

- writing paper
- sentence starters:
  With my eyes I _____.
  With my ears I _____.
  With my nose I _____.
  With my tongue I _____.
  With my hands I _____.

- pictures of eye, nose, hand, tongue, ear
- pencils
- crayons

STUDENT DIRECTIONS

Here's what you'll need:

- paper
- a pencil
- crayons

Here's what you do:

1. Take one paper.
2. Copy each sentence.
3. Finish each sentence with your own words.
4. Illustrate each sentence.

CENTER ACTIVITY PLANNING SHEET

Title: Watch and Listen

Content area(s): Health (five senses) and
Language Arts (listening)*

Purpose: (Introduce)   (Reinforce)   Extend

Objective(s): to strengthen listening comprehension
to introduce information about the
given senses.

Materials:

- filmstrips and tapes
- filmstrip projector and tape player
- evaluation form

STUDENT DIRECTIONS

Here's what you'll need:

- a pencil
- an evaluation form
- filmstrip / tape
- headphones

Here's what you do:

1. Choose one person to turn on the player.
2. Put on your headphones.
3. Turn on the player.
4. Listen and watch.
5. Complete the evaluation form.
6. Rewind the tape.

* This could also be a teacher directed
activity with discussion taking place throughout.

CENTER ACTIVITY PLANNING SHEET

Title: Magic Words

Content area(s): Language Arts (spelling)*

Purpose: Introduce   (Reinforce)   Extend

Objective(s): to practice spelling words

Materials:

- individual word lists
- thinned tempera or water colors
- brushes
- white crayons
- white paper

STUDENT DIRECTIONS

Here's what you'll need:

- your list
- paint
- brush
- white crayon
- white paper

Here's what you do:

1. Take a piece of white paper and a white crayon.
2. Write each of your words using the crayon.
3. Paint over each word.
4. Watch each word appear!

* include other content areas by selecting words from science or social studies, for example.

CENTER ACTIVITY PLANNING SHEET

Title: Write a Story

Content area(s): Language Arts (writing and reading)*

Purpose: Introduce   Reinforce   (Extend)

Objective(s): to write a story that corresponds to a given book jacket

---

Materials:

- lined paper (staple inside of book jackets)
- pencil
- assortment of book jackets (from hard-cover books)

STUDENT DIRECTIONS

Here's what you'll need:

- a book jacket
- a pencil

Here's what you do:

1. Choose one book jacket.
2. Look at the picture carefully.
3. Think about a story that could go with your book jacket.
4. Write your story.

* Depending on the book jackets, you might cover other content areas, too.

CENTER ACTIVITY PLANNING SHEET

Title: Listen to a Story

Content area(s): Language Arts (listening and reading)*

Purpose: Introduce   Reinforce   (Extend)

Objective(s): to strengthen listening comprehension
to practice identifying words
to develop ability to evaluate

Materials:

- tape recorder   • pencils
- headphones
- one storybook cassette tape and accompanying books
- listener's evaluation

STUDENT DIRECTIONS

Here's what you'll need:

- a pencil
- an evaluation form
- a cassette tape
- a book

Here's what you do:

1. Choose one person to turn on the tape recorder.
2. Put on your headphones.
3. Turn on the recorder.
4. Listen to the story and follow along in your book.
5. Complete the evaluation form.
6. Rewind the tape.

* Depending on the title of the book, you might represent other content areas, too.

CENTER ACTIVITY PLANNING SHEET

Title: _Create a Creature_

Content area(s): _Art_

Purpose: (Introduce)   Reinforce   Extend

Objective(s): _to create mirror images_
to design an object

Materials:

- white construction paper
- crayons
- scissors

STUDENT DIRECTIONS

Here's what you'll need:

- your first name
- crayons
- paper
- scissors

Here's what you do:

1. Fold your paper length-wise.
2. Unfold it and write your first name on one half. Use a black crayon.
3. Fold again and rub.
4. Open and trace over the letters.
5. Design a creature using your letter shapes.
6. Cut around your creature.

Michael

CENTER ACTIVITY PLANNING SHEET

Title: _How Many?_

Content area(s): _Mathematics (graphing)_

Purpose: Introduce (Reinforce) Extend

Objective(s): _to practice constructing a bar graph_

Materials:

- pencils
- 9" x 12" construction paper
- container with small pieces of construction paper
- glue

STUDENT DIRECTIONS

Here's what you'll need:

- paper
- large paper
- paper scraps
- glue
- a partner

Here's what you do:

1. Fold your large paper into thirds.
2. Label each section like this:

tables	chairs	doors

3. Count each of these objects in the room.
4. Glue small paper scraps under each column that shows how many of each are in the room.
5. Make sure you and your partner sign your names on the graph.

CENTER ACTIVITY PLANNING SHEET

Title: What's Happening?

Content area(s): Science (plants) / Language Arts (writing)

Purpose: Introduce   Reinforce   (Extend)

Objective(s): to make and record observations
about plant growth

Materials:

- seeds planted in clear containers
- plant journals
- pencils
- crayons

STUDENT DIRECTIONS

Here's what you'll need:

- your seed container
- your plant journal
- a pencil
- crayons

Here's what you do:

1. Look at your seed.
2. Complete each sentence shown below in your journal.
   Today is _____.
   My seed is _____.
3. Draw a picture of what your seed looks like.
4. Color your picture.
5. Compare your seed with others in your group. How is it alike? How is it different?

CENTER ACTIVITY PLANNING SHEET

Title: Create a Comic Conversation

Content area(s): Language Arts (reading and writing)

Purpose: Introduce   Reinforce   (Extend)

Objective(s): to practice sequencing

to write conversation for comics

Materials:

- pencils
- unlined paper
- glue
- comic strips with words removed

STUDENT DIRECTIONS

Here's what you'll need:

- a pencil
- a comic strip with words removed
- paper
- glue

Here's what you do:

1. Choose a comic strip.
2. Glue it on your paper.
3. Write a conversation for each picture.
4. Repeat steps 1-3 if you have time.

CENTER ACTIVITY PLANNING SHEET

Title: _All About Me!_

Content area(s): _Social Studies (self-esteem) and_
Language Arts (speaking)

Purpose: (Introduce)   Reinforce   Extend

Objective(s): _to locate pictures that show_
characteristics of oneself

Materials:

- magazines
- scissors
- construction paper
- glue
- crayons

STUDENT DIRECTIONS

Here's what you'll need:

- magazines
- scissors
- paper
- glue
- crayons

Here's what you do:

1. Look through magazines to find pictures that show things about yourself.
2. Cut out the pictures.
3. Glue the pictures onto the paper.
4. Using a crayon, write "ME" on your poster.
5. Use your poster to tell your group about yourself.

CENTER ACTIVITY PLANNING SHEET

Title: _Make a Map_

Content area(s): _Social Studies (mapping)_

Purpose: Introduce   Reinforce   (Extend)

Objective(s): _to construct a map of the classroom_

Materials:

- unlined paper
- pencil
- crayons

STUDENT DIRECTIONS

Here's what you'll need:

- paper
- pencil
- crayons

Here's what you do:

1. Look around our classroom.
2. Take one paper and pencil.
3. Using what you know about maps, make a map of our room.
4. Label each item on your map.
5. Color you map if you have time.

Special Touches

Keeping in mind that your curriculum is what drives the content of your learning centers, there are ways to create the visual appeal often associated with learning centers without spending endless hours decorating. Here are some timesaving

suggestions, strategies, and tips to enhance your centers. Some, such as the Reading Corner, are designed to last as long as you want. Others can easily be adapted from month to month by changing a few basic details.

Sign Design

Make attractive signs for centers with catchy labels. You might invite children to name their class "publishing company" and create a sign to hang over the writing center. They can add a 3-D element by using pencils, papers, erasers, and other objects associated with the center in their sign.

Bulletin-Board Backdrops

Create bulletin board displays that correspond to the centers. Students can help with this one! If, for example, the center is about sea life, students can create an underwater mural to cover the board. Students can use the board as a backdrop for displaying work they complete at the center.

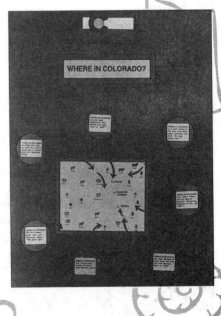

Centers Within Centers

Create special-interest centers by displaying objects related to the topic. For example, in a center exploring ocean life, invite students to share shell collections. For centers on community work-

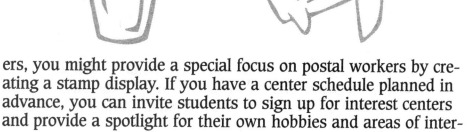

ers, you might provide a special focus on postal workers by creating a stamp display. If you have a center schedule planned in advance, you can invite students to sign up for interest centers and provide a spotlight for their own hobbies and areas of interest.

Cozy Corners

Use see-through wall hangings to create a sense of coziness at your centers while still allowing you to see what's going on in the room. Hang fishnet from the ceiling over the center and down the sides. Or, join the plastic rings that hold six packs of soda together to create dividers. Use pipe cleaners, a glue gun, or staples. Suspend dividers from the ceiling and attach to a low bookshelf below. Clear shower curtains make good dividers, too. Just decorate and hang to create separate center spaces. Suspend clothesline across centers to hang directions and/or student creations, as well to create a sense of separateness.

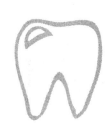

Trinkets and Toys

Collect trinkets that pertain to specific centers. Surprise students at a Spider center with spider rings. Offer magic wands at a Word Wizard center. Supply alphabet rubber stamps for extra fun at a spelling center or dinosaur stamps at a dinosaur center. Teacher supply, toy, and discount stores are all good sources of these small but especially appealing center extras.

Center Personalities

Let your room take on the personality of the centers. For example, if your centers have an Apple theme, create schedule cards in the shape of apples. Make group folder masters (see

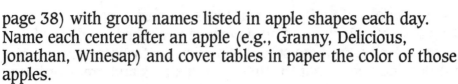

page 38) with group names listed in apple shapes each day. Name each center after an apple (e.g., Granny, Delicious, Jonathan, Winesap) and cover tables in paper the color of those apples.

Environment Enhancers

If space permits, bring in additional furniture that can add special appeal to a center. You might add bean bags, small end tables, and table lamps to a reading center. An old bathtub filled with pillows makes an inviting place to read. An inflatable boat is another good place to read or to display books. Of course, rocking chairs and sofas are fine additions, too.

Details That Delight

To spark student interest, it's not necessary to embellish each of your learning centers with elaborate decor. Just a bit of extra attention to details will help turn drab into dynamite. For example:

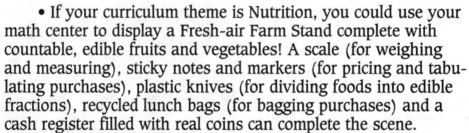

• If your curriculum theme is Nutrition, you could use your math center to display a Fresh-air Farm Stand complete with countable, edible fruits and vegetables! A scale (for weighing and measuring), sticky notes and markers (for pricing and tabulating purchases), plastic knives (for dividing foods into edible fractions), recycled lunch bags (for bagging purchases) and a cash register filled with real coins can complete the scene.

• Your science center can easily double as a Kitchen Test Lab complete with edible science recipes and tasting experiments kids can sink their teeth into. Stock such a center with kid-approved ingredients they can use to prepare no-cook treats, or provide a variety of food samples (cereal, applesauce, yogurt) and prepared response sheets they can use to create consumer response taste-tests.

• Transform your listening center into a concert hall or movie theater by adding a television, a VCR, and video recordings (of ballet performances, classical music presentations, or award-winning literature-based children's films). Be certain to include

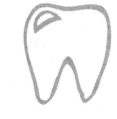

writing and drawing supplies so viewers can record their reactions to viewing experiences. Black tie and popcorn optional.

• Turn your writing center into a Comic Book Store. Use a front-facing wire book rack to display comics (on-loan from students), and provide blank books and drawing supplies so students can write, illustrate, and publish their own comic creations. (Teaching Tip: You can use such a center to explore issues of violence, super heroes, animation, collections, and so on.)

• Turn a ho-hum art center into a Costume Design Studio. Request donations of dress-up clothes, bolts of material, scarves, masks, wigs, hats, jewelry, and other related costuming supplies so students can create costumes for dolls, or, on a larger scale, so they can organize a start-to-finish costume design show based on a curriculum theme (monsters, sports, literary characters, etc.).

Specialized Interest Centers

Apart from adding a little flash to regular learning centers, you can showcase themes with Specialized Interest Centers. A Specialized Interest Center provides an additional area or play space for children to explore theme-related concepts. Here are some ideas to try:

Working Displays

Set up your learning center near a bulletin board or display space and use the arrangement to enhance the center's ambiance (and to lend attractive storage space to your room). For example, if you're working with an Apple theme, use the bulletin board to display a large apple tree with pickable, apple-shaped booklets students can use to record apple facts and stories. (Such booklets may be stored right on the display while in process of being completed!) If you've set up a cooking center, use the wall space to store student-designed cookbooks, showcase recipes, and hang assorted cooking utensils (from around the world). Remember, ask students for their wall design ideas—and then engage their help in putting their ideas to work.

Costumes and Props

Every center idea lends itself to costuming and prop possibilities. Postal workers need adding machines, clipboards, postal stationery supplies, and "uniforms." Restauranteurs need menus, aprons, chef's hats, dinnerware, serving trays, cookware, table settings, and so on. Ask parents and colleagues to lend costumes and props, scour flea markets and garage sales, and check restaurant supply stores (ask if they can donate any damaged but still safe supplies).

Center Structures

A large appliance carton can be reused as the central focus of one learning center after another—or can be used on its own to create a free-standing center. For example, with a little creativity and a bit of paint, a refrigerator carton can be painted to resemble a doughnut shop, repainted to resemble a rocket ship and repainted again to represent a grass hut. To help the carton easily change from one play space to another, just use a fresh coat of whitewash to "erase" the old painted-on details, let dry, and have students add new details with tempera paints.

Stocking Your Centers

The following companies are among those that provide commercially prepared activities, supplies, and teacher resource. books.

Creative Teaching Press
P.O. Box 6017
Cypress, CA 90630-0017
(800) 444-4CTP

The Education Center, Inc.
1607 Battleground Ave.
P.O. Box 9753
Greensboro, NC 27408
(800) 334-0298

Educational Insights
19560 S. Rancho Way
Dominguez Hills, CA 90220
(800) 933-3277

Evan-Moor Corporation
18 Lower Ragsdale Dr.
Monterey, CA 93940
(800) 777-4489

Fearon Teacher Aids
P.O. Box 280
Carthage, IL 62321
(800) 242-7272

Good Apple
P.O. Box 299
Carthage, IL 62321-0299
(800) 435-7234

Heinemann
361 Hanover St.
Portsmouth, NH 03801-3959
(800) 541-2086

Scholastic Inc.
P.O. Box 7502
Jefferson City,
MO 65102-9968
(800) 325-6149

Teacher Created Materials
6421 Industry Way
Westminster, CA 92683-3608
(800) 662-4321

Teacher Ideas Press
P.O. Box 6633
Englewood, CO 80155-6633

T.S. Denison
9601 Newton Ave. S
Minneapolis, MN 55431
(800) 328-3831

The Wright Group
19201 120th Ave. NE
Bothell, WA 98011-9512
(800) 345-6073

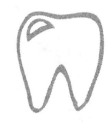

Books that provide additional ideas include:

Story Stretchers for the Primary Grades by R. Canaday and S. Raines (Gryphon House)
This book provides a wealth of ideas for using children's books and includes activities for writing and other centers.

Designing Groupwork by E. Cohen (Teachers College Press)
Provides strategies and activities for helping children learn to work in groups.

I Can Make a Rainbow by M. Frank (Incentive)
Describes art activities and lists specific ideas for using different techniques to create pictures and objects.

Learning Centers for Young Children (3rd ed.) (Gryphon House)
Offers a collection of learning center ideas and tips for management.

Change for Children by S. Kaplan, J. Kaplan, S. Madsen, and B. Gould (Scott, Foresman)
Provides several ideas for learning centers and additional ideas for individualizing learning.

Science on a Shoestring by A. Strongin (Addison-Wesley)
Offers several science activities suitable for centers that can be completed with few supplies and materials.

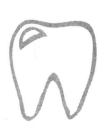

CHAPTER 6

Questions And Answers

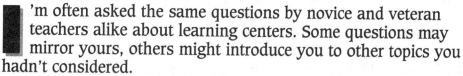
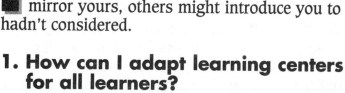

'm often asked the same questions by novice and veteran teachers alike about learning centers. Some questions may mirror yours, others might introduce you to other topics you hadn't considered.

1. How can I adapt learning centers for all learners?

The way you adapt a center will depend on the learners and your purpose for using the center. For example, to provide for varying abilities with reading, you might use both pictures and words when writing directions. You could also record directions on a cassette tape.

If one major purpose for using a center is to have students learn from one another, you might decide to group learners of varying abilities together. To accommodate varying abilities, offer activity choices that range from very concrete to more abstract. Permit students to work at their own pace.

Finally, by providing open-ended activities, you automatically allow for differences in your students. For example, you might have a spelling center in which each child completes activities related to individualized spelling lists.

2. How many centers do I need?

How you intend to use learning centers will help you answer this question. If you intend to have a center time in which all students are expected to go to a center, you will want to have enough centers to accommodate all learners without crowding. Thus, if you have thirty students and you want no

more than five students at a center at a given time, you would need to have six centers. To answer this question, then, determine how many students you want to have working together and make sure you have enough centers to make this possible.

3. How many students should be at a center?

Regardless of how I have used learning centers, I have found one to five students per center to be ideal. More than six usually poses problems, usually because of space and materials. Imagine, if you will, eight children in the block center trying to construct various objects as opposed to four. There is only so much space (and so many blocks)!

4. How often do I need to change the centers?

Changing centers and/or the activities within a center really depends on how you use centers. For example, if centers provide a structure for delivering curriculum and students are grouped and expected to rotate to given centers on a daily basis, the center itself would not need to change but the activities would. If, on the other hand, students choose from several activities within a center, changing the activities would not necessarily have to occur on a daily basis.

If you use centers in a supplemental way, with students completing them at their own pace as they have time, you might only need to change centers on a weekly, bi-weekly, or monthly basis. You'll want to pay close attention to how many students have completed a given center to determine in advance when you'll need to change the activities.

5. What's a good time limit for a center?

Generally, I have found that anywhere from twenty to forty minutes gives students enough time to complete centers as they are described in this book. However, the exact time limit will depend on age level, student interest, available time, and other factors. Some words of caution are in order, though.

First, if students are grouped and expected to rotate from center to center on a given schedule, make sure that the activities at the various centers take about the same length of time to

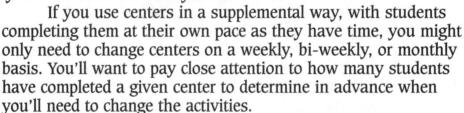

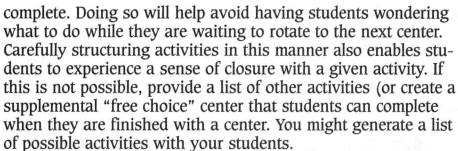

complete. Doing so will help avoid having students wondering what to do while they are waiting to rotate to the next center. Carefully structuring activities in this manner also enables students to experience a sense of closure with a given activity. If this is not possible, provide a list of other activities (or create a supplemental "free choice" center that students can complete when they are finished with a center. You might generate a list of possible activities with your students.

Second, if centers include open-ended activities that may require more time to complete, make sure your schedule reflects this time requirement. If changing the time schedule presents too many problems, provide students with places to safely store unfinished projects.

Third, regardless of how you use centers, plan time for cleaning up and rotating to the next centers into your time table. I have found five minutes to be an optimum amount of time for this transition.

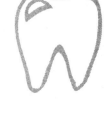

6. Should all centers focus on the same theme?

If you want them to! Again, the answer to this question depends on your purpose for using centers. If your main objective is to integrate centers into the curriculum, you may find yourself setting up several science centers, all of which students are expected to complete. However, within each center, you may highlight aspects of language arts and other subject areas. Say you want to teach about the five senses. Your centers might work like this:

• One center might offer students a choice of books about the five senses. At another center they may construct stories about how they use each sense on a given day.

• At another center students might choose words related to the five senses that they would like to learn to spell.

• At yet another center students might construct a dictionary in which they record words about the five senses as their study progresses.

7. How do you motivate students to use learning centers?

Probably the best way to motivate students is to use their interests whenever possible. If, for example, they are interested in clowns, you might be able to achieve several of your curriculum goals by exploring this topic.

Asking students to contribute to the center is another way to motivate them. I remember asking students to bring in seeds or pictures of seeds from home to contribute to our plant center. We used the pictures for a bulletin board display and examined the seeds for likenesses and differences.

After you have used centers for a while and feel comfortable with them, you might also want to have students actually create a center, complete with activities. This would be an excellent way for students to show understanding of a topic they have been researching or one which they know and enjoy. For example, students who collect baseball cards as a hobby could create a center that would teach others in the class how to read a card and how to determine its value. You could provide students with center activity sheets (see page 36) and instruct them on how to use them.

Still another way to motivate student use is to provide choices within the centers. As a result of being able to choose, students may feel more ownership over their learning and more motivated as a result.

Generally, though, I have not found motivation to be an issue. Instead, I have found that students like to complete centers. As stated earlier, however, remember that most students need to be taught how to make choices and how to work independently.

8. What grade levels are learning centers appropriate for?

Preschool through college, I have found that learning centers help learners to be more actively engaged and that their learning is maximized as a result.

9. Where can I get the materials to use in my centers?

Begin by taking another look at everyday objects that are often discarded such as egg cartons, tissue tubes, cardboard boxes of various sizes, and laundry detergent jugs. Often times these materials can be used to create activities to use within centers. For example, an egg carton becomes a matching activity, a cardboard box covered with contact paper becomes a storage bin for books. If you have a lot of baby food jars, as I did at one time, with a little imagination you will find several ways to use them. One word of warning, however: Once you start "relooking" at objects, make sure you have plenty of storage space!

Also remember the teaching guides at your disposal. These guides can provide a wealth of ideas that require few extra materials. Finally, there are many commercial resources available to assist you, funds permitting.

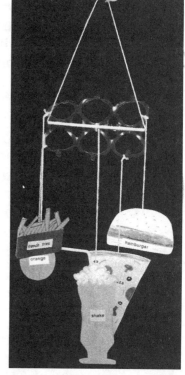

10. What's the best way to begin using learning centers?

If you've ever watched people at a swimming pool, you've probably noticed that some enter the water gradually whereas others dive in. Implementing learning centers is much the same. Some choose to begin slowly, using a few centers each week that primarily reinforce what students have learned. Others begin by using learning centers as a way of delivering content. They have students rotate from center to center and change centers frequently to accommodate changes in the curriculum. The answer to this question, then, brings us full circle, back to the introduction in which I stated the importance of setting yourself up for success. Pace yourself to allow this to happen.

NOTES

NOTES